The Second Reform Act

IN THE SAME SERIES

General Editors: Eric J. Evans and P.D. King

LANCASTER PAMPHLETS

The Second Reform Act

John K. Walton

London

First published in 1983 by
Methuen & Co. Ltd

Reprinted 1993, 1996 by
Routledge
11 New Fetter Lane, London EC4P 4EE

Typeset in Great Britain by
Scarborough Typesetting Services
and printed by
Clays Ltd, St Ives plc

British Library Cataloguing in Publication Data
Walton, John K.
The Second Reform Act. – (Lancaster pamphlets)
1. Great Britain. Parliament – Reform
2. Representative government and representation
– Great Britain – History – 19th century
I. Title II. Series
328.41'0734   JN543

ISBN 0–415–10432–7

Contents

Acknowledgements

I should like to thank those members of my special subject class on mid-Victorian England who have tolerated my interest in the Second Reform Act while (usually) asking for as much social history and as little political history as I was prepared to allow them. Thanks also to Eric Evans and David King for their editorial work, and to Mike Winstanley for characteristically useful and relevant suggestions. Thanks especially to Jenny Smith, who has read this pamphlet twice in typescript to check for fluency and comprehensibility, and as a result knows far more about the Second Reform Act than she can have imagined in her wildest nightmares. The results are nobody's fault but my own.

JKW

Foreword

Lancaster Pamphlets offer concise and up-to-date accounts of major historical topics, primarily for the help of students preparing for Advanced Level examinations, though they should also be of value to those pursuing introductory courses in universities and other institutions of higher education. Without being all-embracing, their aims are to bring some of the central themes or problems confronting students and teachers into sharper focus than the textbook writer can hope to do; to provide the reader with some of the results of recent research which the textbook may not embody; and to stimulate thought about the whole interpretation of the topic under discussion.

At the end of this pamphlet is a list of works, most of them recent or fairly recent, which the writer considers most important for those who wish to study the subject further.

1

The importance of
the Second Reform Act

The Reform Act of 1867 was highly controversial at the time and has remained so ever since. However we look at the political history of nineteenth-century Britain, its importance in signposting and bringing about changes of direction, and in bringing new forces into play, is second only to that of its illustrious precursor of 1832. When we remember that the introduction of the secret ballot in 1872 followed hard on its heels, the mid-Victorian changes in the electoral system can be made to look potentially revolutionary; and we shall see that that is how many contemporaries saw them.

Reform in 1867 considerably increased the number of potential and actual voters; it enfranchised large numbers of urban working men; it redistributed seats in ways that had complex and important implications; and its detailed provisions stimulated the political parties into new systems of organization at the local level, as they tried to build bridges to the new voters and devise ways of satisfying and accommodating them. After 1867 significant changes took place in constitutional practice, in the working of the party system, in the content of legislative programmes and above all in the nature of the relationship between politicians and an expanded electorate. How far these changes were in some sense caused by the Second Reform Act, and how far they were responses to the deeper social and political currents which put a further measure of reform on the political agenda and helped it to come to pass, is a matter of debate. At a more superficial level, the banker, economic journalist and political commentator Walter Bagehot was able to argue at the time that the post-1867 change in the political climate had more to do with the death of Palmerston in 1865, and the advent of a new generation of political leaders, than with the Reform Act. It is one thing to say what the Reform Act did; it is quite another, more interesting and more difficult thing to say what its wider influence was.

The Second Reform Act has in some senses been the 'poor relation' of the first. It was not a major constitutional breakthrough in the same way, although its passing confirmed a long-growing and by then almost universal consensus that the 1832 Act could not be expected to remain fixed and unchanging. The circumstances of its passing were less dramatic. Despite the vehement language of some campaigners for reform, and the Hyde Park meetings which aroused transitory fears of revolution in some influential quarters, the reform campaign could not match the revolutionary overtones of 1832. Even Karl Marx, eagerly looking for revolutionary portents from his vantage point in the British Museum Reading Room, found little to encourage him in this respect. There was drama enough within parliament, but there was no real external threat to the constitution. Moreover, the 1867 settlement held the stage for a shorter time that that of 1832, for its provisions were to be altered again in the further reform and redistribution of 1884–5. But the importance of the Second Reform Act is indisputable. Contemporaries discussed its implications with fascination and concern, and it has given rise to fierce debate among historians, who disagree about the significance of its timing, nature and long-term consequences.

Very few historians, no doubt, would now see the Second Reform Act in the old Whiggish way, as another inevitable step on the road to a workable democracy and to the ultimate refinement of the perfect British constitution, for eventual export to less happy lands. That kind of innocence is no longer with us. Rather more might interpret it as an essential element in a long-term process of judicious concession and subtle management by which the established ruling class of nineteenth-century England

2

justified and perpetuated its rule. From that perspective, Royden Harrison argues that the British working class, increasingly 'respectable' and well organized, and still retaining some 'revolutionary potentialities', had 'attained precisely that level of development at which it was safe to concede its enfranchisement and dangerous to withhold it' (1965, 133). On this basis, the Second Reform Act defused a revival of working-class unrest and gave potential revolutionaries a trusted place in the workings of the constitution, attaching their loyalty firmly to a system which had been reformed to accommodate them. But this approach glosses over the changing balance between the landed aristocracy and gentry and the industrial and commercial middle classes in mid-Victorian parliaments, and it imparts a taint of conspiracy to the proceedings which would have been very difficult to organize in practice. Nevertheless, the idea that those in authority were prepared to expand the political nation to embrace a much wider working-class electorate, to prevent working-class frustrations from threatening political stability, helps to explain the passing of a measure of parliamentary reform in the late 1860s or early 1870s. What it does not explain is the nature of the legislation, or the way in which it came about.

Perhaps the most peculiar aspects of the 1867 Reform Act are that it was concocted and obtained by a Conservative minority government in an era of sustained Liberal ascendancy, and that it went much further in a democratic direction than had the Liberal measure of the previous year, which was thrown out by a combined opposition of Tories and dissident right-wing Whigs. The key to this enigma is to be found in the political skills and personal attributes of Disraeli, who was, above all, responsible for the controversially far-reaching extension of the franchise which the Act embodied. How should we interpret his actions? Was he gambling, perhaps irresponsibly, with the stability of the constitution in the hope of winning a tactical victory for himself and for his party, with no real idea of the likely or even the possible longer-term consequences of his concessions? Or were his admittedly consummate tactical skills harnessed, with conscious foresight, to the remaking of the Conservative Party in a new and successful populist guise, reaching out to the urban working-class voter in a way that

3

was to alter the balance of political forces, in England at least, for a generation to come? These questions about Disraeli, the Conservative Party and reform are central to our understanding of why the Second Reform Act came when it did and was as it was; and our answers to them also affect our interpretation of long-term trends in British politics until the turn of the century and beyond. However, before we take a longer look at the impact of the 1867 Reform Act we need to be clear about the background to and circumstances of its passing, and precisely how it changed the rules and re-defined the playing area of the political game.

2

The making of the
Second Reform Act

The demand for a further measure of parliamentary reform had never been completely stilled from the moment that the nature of the compromise settlement of 1832 became apparent. The radical advocates of manhood suffrage saw the First Reform Act as a sellout by the more moderate and pragmatic reformers, and at best they viewed it as a short-term, interim arrangement which would soon have to give way to a much fuller package of democratic reform. The legislative programmes and social attitudes of the first post-Reform parliaments confirmed the radicals' worst suspicions, and a combination of trade depression, repressive policies towards trade unions and the poor, and apparent indifference to working-class grievances enabled the Chartists to enlist a mass following at times of stress in the late 1830s and early 1840s. The Charter's Six Points envisaged more accountable, accessible and socially representative parliaments as well as manhood suffrage, and its supporters included believers in each man's natural right to vote, or in the need to rediscover a 'lost' democratic Old English constitution, as well as those who were more concerned to see their interests served and their living standards protected by a radically reformed parliament.

The enactment of the People's Charter would have provided a much more far-reaching transformation of parliament and constitution than the Second Reform Act eventually produced. But despite attempted uprisings in 1839, followed by what some see as a 'revolutionary general strike' in 1842 and ultimately by the famous mass meeting on Kennington Common in 1848, the Chartists never came anywhere near to success, whether by constitutional or insurrectionary means. After 1848 they never regained their mass support, which had always been intermittent and uncertain; and although they remained strong through most of the 1850s in northern textile towns such as Halifax, the hoped-for revival never came. As economic conditions improved and governments became more responsive to pressure for economic and social reform, working-class reformers and their middle-class allies concentrated their attention increasingly on narrower and more readily attainable goals. They campaigned against specific privileges of the aristocracy or the Church of England, or in support of free trade and cheap government. They sought to make the working classes worthy of the vote by promoting education, Nonconformity or the temperance movement. Those who retained a commitment to parliamentary reform became less demanding in their hopes and expectations. During the 1850s Chartism was gradually superseded by a more heterogeneous band of moderate reformers who concentrated increasingly on cultivating an image of respectability and willingness to work within the existing constitutional and economic system. Under these less fraught conditions, mainstream politicians found themselves able to put a further instalment of reform on the agenda, to bring the 'respectable working man' within the bounds of the political nation. We must not forget that the reform debates of 1866 and 1867 were only the latest and most eloquent of a sequence of discussions on the propriety and practicability of a further extension of the franchise.

Limited reform proposals were regular features of the parliaments of the 1850s. Most of them emanated from Lord John Russell, who had rashly and impulsively pronounced in 1837 against any further measure of reform, but by 1848 he was already toying with as cautious widening of voting rights in the boroughs. As Prime Minister in 1849 he floated a proposal to enfranchise £5 householders in the boroughs and £20 tenants in the counties, but his Cabinet expressed such profound indifference that the scheme never surfaced in parliament. In 1852 he managed to introduce a similar bill, which also envisaged some merging of the smallest borough seats; but his ministry was disintegrating and the Earl of Granville professed himself alone among Russell's Cabinet colleagues in venturing 'to hint that I was not in perfect despair at there being such as thing as a Reform Bill'. This proposal proved abortive; Marx unkindly remarked that it was 'of such Lilliputian features that neither the Conservatives thought it worthwhile to attack nor the Liberals to support it'. Meanwhile, Russell himself would have nothing to do with the regular proposals for the secret ballot and for more far-reaching measures of reform which emanated from the radical fringes of the House of Commons.

Russell continued to tinker with reform, with little enthusiasm from colleagues, parliament or the outside world. Edward Ellice, the veteran Liberal MP for Coventry, argued to Lord Stanley in 1854 that 'no small measure of reform ever can pass – it must be large, or it will not rouse interest enough to overcome obstacles'. In December 1853 Disraeli had expressed not dissimilar sentiments from a different perspective: 'He objected to reform, thinking you could not find any point to stop at short of the absolute sovereignty of the people.' But he was not consistent in this regard: at other times, and even as early as 1848, he could see possible advantages in a future extension of the franchise. In 1859, he was the moving spirit behind the appearance of a Conservative reform bill which demonstrated the emergence of a widening acceptance among the political élite of the expediency, and even the need, of further moderate reform. Even Palmerston, no friend to even the most limited concessions to democracy, had made grudgingly encouraging noises two years previously.

The Conservative proposal of 1859 was purely a matter of political expediency. It aimed at equalizing the county and borough franchises, and compelling voters living in urban constituencies to vote in their borough rather than in the county, in an attempt to make the county seats safer for rural Conservatism. Accordingly, 70 seats were to be transferred from small boroughs, 52 of them to the counties and 18 to the larger towns. Nothing was offered to the urban artisan except indirectly through the proposed 'fancy franchises', as the radical industrialist MP John Bright contemptuously called them, which would have given votes to men who had £60 accumulated in a savings bank or £10 per year from government stock. This device, invented by Russell in 1854, was indeed an illusory concession, and there was dissent in Cabinet even over this cautiously opportunistic package. It was not difficult for the Liberal leadership to mobilize opposition from left and right to defeat the bill, coming as it did from a minority government.

The failure of the bill was greeted with resounding apathy, and little more interest was taken in the snuffing out of a further Russell scheme in 1860. The reform question was then shelved for several years, even by Russell himself, though not by Bright and his allies. Before we examine the revival of a lively debate on the reform issue in the mid-1860s, we need to account for the strange episode of 1859–60. Why, when senior politicians of all hues were agreed that reform had become an inescapable commitment in the late 1850s, did the damp squibs of 1859 and 1860 fizzle out with so little fuss, within parliament and outside it?.

This is a surprisingly difficult question. Despite Bright's efforts to stir up a campaign for a major extension of urban voting rights in 1859, which 'aroused considerable enthusiasm in Birmingham, Manchester and Glasgow, but not enough to disturb the House of Commons' (F. B. Smith 1966, 40), there was no new pressure from without for reform. Some concern was expressed at the need to iron out anomalies and make the system more defensible in a time of prosperity and quiet, to pre-empt a probable future campaign for radical reform which might be difficult to resist; and this point of view was espoused by several right-wing Liberals and Whigs who later helped to bring down the Liberal bill of 1866 on the grounds that it tried to go too far. Most important, perhaps, was the difficult balance of power between the parties and factions which complicated mid-Victorian politics. Party discipline was weak, and there were many maverick MPs and floating voters. The emergent Liberal Party, though invariably the largest parliamentary grouping, was an uneasy and deeply divided coalition, and like the Conservatives its leaders were normally dependent on support from the radicals if their governments were to survive for

8

any length of time. Promises of reform were a way of securing radical goodwill, although the measures on offer never came up to expectations, and a well-managed change in the electoral rules, involving a careful redistribution of seats, might tip the balance in favour of the party which succeeded in bringing it about, enabling it to secure genuine and lasting majorities. These perceptions were perhaps particularly acute in the late 1850s, at a time of relative prosperity when judicious concessions to the respectable working-class voter seemed potentially less threatening than hitherto, putting reform on the agenda of both parties. On both sides, however, there were plenty of faint-hearts and principled opponents of franchise extension, and their fears and objections set narrow limits to the range of options which were available to policy-makers. When it became clear that neither side could obtain its preferred measure of reform, the issue could be allowed to slumber for a few years longer. The ascendancy of Palmerston, whose priorities most definitely lay elsewhere, merely deepened its repose.

But spry as he was, even the octogenarian Palmerston could not live for ever, and when he died in 1865 the sleeping giant was already stirring again. Even so, it would be misleading to make too much of the renewed pressure for reform. With hindsight, the most important development might seem to be Gladstone's conversion to a much fuller, though subtly qualified, extension of the working-class electorate in May 1864, at a time when he was becoming an increasingly popular politician and an obvious candidate for the highest office. But Sir Charles Wood, a fellow member of Palmerston's Cabinet, set matters in an intriguing contemporary perspective when he discussed Gladstone's speech with Lord Stanley a few days later:

He disapproves Gladstone's speech strongly, though agreeing that the language is so vague as to pledge him to nothing: thinks however that it indicates no settled conviction, but is only one of Gladstone's odd inexplicable freaks: would not be surprised if he were to make another speech in an opposite sense next week . . . the agitation cannot be revived for the present, and if tried will only damage the Liberal party.   (Vincent 1978, 217)

In the short run, Wood was correct on the last two counts. Reform was hardly an issue in the 1865 General Election. It was only aired in a few constituencies where radical candidates brandished their commitment to it. When it was revived, it did indeed damage the Liberal Party, driving a wedge between the aristocratic Whig defenders of the landed interest and the radicals. Its reappearance on the agenda followed the death of Palmerston and the beginning of Lord John Russell's final stint as Prime Minister, now operating from the House of Lords as Earl Russell, a title which had been conferred on him in 1861. But Russell's campaign manager was Gladstone, whose conversion to reform was more principled, more thoroughgoing, more lasting and more serious than Wood and most of his other colleagues had imagined.

This is not to say that Gladstone had been converted to the full reform programme of manhood suffrage and the secret ballot, which had practically no support in parliament anyway. But, on this issue as on others, he had come a long way from his reactionary Tory origins, and he was willing to see the right to vote extended to those independent, respectable, thrifty, literate members of the upper working class who had reasonable housing, steady work and a nest-egg in the savings bank or Co-operative Society which gave them a stake in the existing social system and made them likely to be politically trustworthy. He had been particularly impressed by the stoical endurance of sustained privation which had been shown by the Lancashire cotton workers during the interruption to their trade at the time of the American Civil War, when prolonged unemployment and near-starvation had brought no threat to property and order. Here, it seemed, was a worthy stratum of the working class which was fit to be entrusted with the vote.

The belief that there existed a 'safe' top layer of working-class town-dwellers who could be admitted to constitutional privileges without threatening the rule of landed property was quite widespread among the mid-Victorian governing class. It provided a measure of justification for the various abortive reform bills of 1852–61, especially as an extended urban franchise could be coupled with an increased number of seats for the counties in which the aristocracy and gentry could continue to rule the roost through their influence on tenants and tradesmen. Liberals and democrats could be appeased, without the whole constitutional edifice and power structure being threatened. The key problem was, where should the line be drawn in establishing a new urban voting qualification? How far below the existing £10 householder franchise was it safe to go? There had been much debate on this matter when previous reform bills had been framed; and when Gladstone and Russell embarked on a new measure in 1866 they were immediately faced with the same difficulty. The vote was a trust and a privilege, which had to be earned, rather than a right which came naturally. How could one discriminate between the deserving worker who was fit to vote, and the dissolute worker who might be amenable to bribery or, worse still, might vote for a candidate who put working-class interests first and engaged in class warfare against his betters?

The Reform Bill of 1866 differed remarkably little in principle from its predecessors. It still had to walk the tightrope between radical aspirations and Whig forebodings, and its framers had to restrain themselves from threatening to redistribute too many small borough seats away from the control of their own supporters. The key difference was that its promoters pursued their goal with an altogether novel tenacity and drive; and in the process they aroused an opposition within their own party which ultimately forced the resignation of the Russell government, opening the way for the Conservative ministry which was to pass the 1867 Act itself.

The drafting of the 1866 proposal was left largely to Gladstone. There was never any question of the voting qualification in the boroughs falling below 'a clear annual value of £6' per year, firmly excluding the occupants of the poorest housing; but it was not at all clear what this, or any other, figure would mean in practice. The calculation of the number of potential working-class voters was complicated by the wide divergence between house values based on rates and those based on rents, and there were considerable variations in values between towns and between different parts of the country, while local variations in legal practices were also capable of making a big difference to voting rights. The question of whether potential voters paid their own rates, or had them paid for them by the landlord, was particularly important in this respect. The more cautious members of Russell's cabinet, realizing the difficulties and also hoping to postpone decision-making on this thorny and threatening topic for as long as possible, proposed to await the report of a commission of enquiry; but their objections were set aside.

Statistics were gathered as discussion proceeded, however, and the findings proved increasingly disquieting to the Whigs. It was impossible to predict with anything resembling accuracy how many new voters might be added with different rental or rating qualifications, but it was clear that a very large number of houses fell into the band between a £6 annual value and the existing borough limit of £10. Five days before the bill was introduced, a minority of the Cabinet took a deep breath and decided to specify a £7 annual rental as the basis for the urban franchise. Two days later, evidence was presented to show that in 116 boroughs in England and Wales, more than a quarter of the electorate was already 'working-class', although this category was itself difficult to define. This cut the ground from under Gladstone's feet, because it suggested that the working-class élite was already qualifying for the vote in impressive numbers under the existing system. Opponents of reform could ask all the more forcibly, 'Why change at all?' When Gladstone introduced the bill on 12 March, 'with unwonted diffidence', he was offering a hastily concocted measure, based on admittedly inadequate information, and with opinion in most of Russell's predominantly aristocratic Cabinet ranging from the sceptical to the downright hostile.

Apart from the £7 householders in the boroughs, a franchise which Gladstone emphasized as being intended to include 'the artisans and skilled labourers of our towns' but not 'the peasantry or mere hand labourers', the 1866 Bill offered the vote to occupiers of houses and land worth £14 per year (instead of £50) in the counties, with lodgers paying £10 per year in the boroughs, and holders of £50 savings bank deposits in the counties also having the opportunity to register. F. B. Smith's summary suggests that the vote would be extended to one man in four instead of one in five, with the working class still accounting for fewer than half of the borough voters, and a much lower proportion in the counties.

This was hardly a Gadarene rush to democracy, and there was disappointment among radicals at the limited scope of the bill, coupled with recognition that the current House of Commons seemed unlikely to go any further towards the goal of household suffrage and the ballot. Indeed, there was plenty of disquiet on the other side, and ample scope for the bill to be ambushed by the opponents of reform. Enough Whiggish Liberals of Palmerstonian pedigree were unconvinced of the need for reform, and worried about possible consequences, for a combination with the Conservatives to prove fatal to the bill's chances. Ultimately, this is what happened. A group of right-wing Liberals, fortified by the eloquence of the former don, barrister and *The Times* leader writer Robert Lowe, attacked the extension of the franchise as unnecessary for good government and threatening to constitutional stability. They were mocked by Bright as the 'Adullamites', an allusion to the Old Testament story of the Cave of Adullam which housed 'everyone that was in distress . . . and everyone that was discontented'. But once Disraeli had overcome the inertia of the Conservatives' ageing, gouty official leader, the fourteenth Earl of Derby, and mobilized the party against the bill, the Adullamites were able to marshal sufficient support at key moments to ensure its eventual defeat. First, the Adullamites and leading Conservatives collaborated to force the government into combining the redistribution of parliamentary seats with their franchise reforms, instead of taking these complex but interrelated issues in turn. After much wrangling, the Cabinet produced a controversial redistribution proposal which would have transferred 49 seats from small boroughs, 26 of them going to the counties and 15 to industrial towns and the larger English boroughs. Other small boroughs were to be grouped together to form larger and less corruptible constituencies. This proposal would have tipped the electoral balance further towards the Liberals, but it also threatened the constituencies of several of their current supporters, and provided further recruits for the opposition campaign. A series of attacks on the details and principles of the bill followed, as Disraeli tried to generate the maximum

13

support for the most damaging breach; and he was fortified by Conservative fears that a wider county franchise would let in so many urban Liberal tradesmen, immune to the influences of landed society, that seats would be lost and elections become prohibitively expensive. On 18 June Dunkellin's amendment, which proposed that the borough voting qualification should be based on payment of rates rather than rental value, made the bill untenable. Russell's government resigned and a Conservative minority administration took over.

Despite the high quality of much of the parliamentary oratory, and the deep concern expressed by opponents of the democratic principle, parliamentary reform had not been uppermost in the minds of most MPs until the drama of the closing stages of the discussion. The cattle plague, the budget and foreign affairs had been equally engrossing. By 10 June, however, Lord Stanley could assert that, 'The political excitement among the upper classes is greater than it has been for the last seven or eight years.' But he added, 'I do not believe that it is shared to any considerable extent by the people.'

This belief would have been much harder to sustain a fortnight later. The serious reformers among the lower middle and upper working classes had followed the debates assiduously in the rapidly-burgeoning cheap newspaper press of the 1860s, and the defeat of Gladstone and his bill unleashed a wave of angry meetings, demonstrations and denunciations. The Reform League, with its leadership composed of intellectuals and trade unionists with a leavening of manufacturers, began to attract numerous support for its Trafalgar Square meetings, and in late July the famous confrontations took place over the right to hold reform meetings in Hyde Park. The 'riots' hardly deserve the name: at the most fraught moment the park railings seem to have given way under pressure rather than been torn up, and the League's leaders showed a clear and overriding anxiety to restore an order which was never under serious threat. Bright and others might occasionally have used implicitly threatening language at public meetings, but what little damage was done seems to have come from a hooligan fringe, and foreign revolutionaries received short shrift when they tried to encourage violent uprising. Marx told Engels that if the railings – and it was touch and go – had been used offensively and defensively against the police, and about twenty of the latter had been knocked dead, the military would have had to 'intervene' instead of only parading. And then there would have been some fun. (1934, 213)

But this piece of wishful thinking was a tailpiece to a letter which was mainly concerned with the Austro-Prussian war. Marx knew enough about the respectable and constitutional preoccupations of the Reform League's leaders, and about the lack of revolutionary sentiment among the working class at large, to be only too well aware of the limited significance of the Hyde Park affair.

This point is important because the rest of the period leading up to the Second Reform Act was marked by a sustained groundswell of extra-parliamentary pressure, with regular mass meetings and demonstrations in London and the provinces in conscious imitation of the alliance between the radical middle class and the politically-conscious workers which had made a settlement inescapable in 1832. Royden Harrison, in particular, has argued that this pressure from without pushed the new Conservative government into taking up reform, and helped to condition the surprisingly far-reaching nature of the eventual Act. At best, this argument seems overstated. As Cowling remarks, 'The passage of the Reform Act in 1867 was effected in a context of public agitation: it cannot be explained as a simple consequence' (1967, 3). Disraeli seems already to have been considering reform before the Hyde Park disturbances, although the dating of the crucial letter is uncertain. What is clear is that there was no rush to embrace reform during the summer. When Derby wrote to Disraeli on 16 September that 'I am coming reluctantly to the conclusion that we shall have to deal with the question of Reform', the new Prime Minister may have been influenced, as Blake suggests, by 'the growing strength of the Reform movement in the country, the numerous orderly but determined mass meetings addressed by Bright and other popular orators' (1969, 450). But short-term calculations of party political advantage, the extent to which reform was already on the agenda (to the

15

point that the Queen herself was expressing anxiety for a settlement), and the recognition that concessions now would reduce the scope for further and increasing grievance and agitation in the world beyond Westminster, were all of much more account as the saga of the Second Reform Act unfolded; and the first of these themes was probably the most important.

Derby and Disraeli were in a difficult position when they took office. Theirs was a minority government, and all the more so because they were unable – and ultimately unwilling – to coalesce with the Adullamites. Palmerston's majority of 1865 had splintered in reaction to the 1866 Reform Bill, but it was still all too capable of bringing down a rival government. Disraeli's position, moreover, was threatened by an intransigent group of squirearchical right-wing die-hards led by the Marquess of Bath. The party had spent a generation in the political wilderness. It could neither refuse office nor, once the responsibility had been accepted, afford to sit back passively and wait to be ousted by a reconstituted Liberal government. With or without the external agitation, reform of some sort would have been difficult to dodge.

Despite these circumstances, the Conservative leadership moved slowly. There was much debate about how far to go how fast; and Disraeli was at first particularly reluctant to act. During the last months of 1866, Derby's plan to introduce a series of vague Resolutions on the form a desirable reform might take, rather than a specific bill, was discussed in Cabinet and adopted. But a Royal Commission was then envisaged, ostensibly to provide further information but really as a delaying tactic. As F. B. Smith points out, the thirteen clauses which Derby and Disraeli drafted, and which were accepted by the Cabinet on 8 November, 'set out all the principles that were needful for a Bill and made a Commission superfluous' (1966, 139). Blake suggests that 'Throughout the winter Disraeli and Derby were principally concerned to procrastinate. They were anxious to take the initiative away from the Liberals, but they wanted to postpone legislation' (1969, 452). It was partly to find 'a really sticky, vaguely practicable question with which to clog the Commission's deliberations', as F. B. Smith puts it, that Derby came up with the idea of household suffrage as the basic urban franchise, hedged around with restrictions and coupled with plural votes for favoured categories of the propertied and respectable. A similar proposal formed the core of the Reform Bill which was eventually introduced on 18 March 1867. But a large number of peculiar things had happened in the meantime.

Parliament reconvened after the Christmas vacation on 5 February. Between then and 18 March the original timetable of Resolutions, Royal Commission and reform in 1868, after a decent interval, had been cast to the winds. In their anxiety to preempt any further Liberal initiative, and if possible to widen the split in the Liberal ranks, while holding a suspicious Cabinet together and safeguarding the ideal of a balanced constitution with no predominant position for a single class – and least of all the working class – Derby and Disraeli underwent the most remarkable gyrations. Increasingly, Disraeli took the centre of the stage, as he piloted his party through the Commons discussions, impelled by the need to protect his own place in the party hierarchy, the hope of securing a parliamentary victory on a key issue which might rehabilitate the party's fortunes for the future, and the personal pleasure to be derived from outsmarting Gladstone.

Blake summarizes the course of events in all its bewildering complexity. Household suffrage based on payment of rates in person (which would disqualify a large number of voters who would have qualified on the basis of rent alone), and compensated by 'fancy franchises', was proposed in Cabinet on 6 February but abandoned on 9 February, after General Peel had threatened a damaging resignation. The leisurely route via Resolutions and a Royal Commission was dropped the day after it was introduced into parliament, and the Resolutions procedure was itself abandoned on 26 February. Meanwhile, three different proposals for new borough franchises had been brandished at a puzzled House. Three Cabinet ministers, Cranborne and Carnarvon as well as Peel, resigned on 2 March when it became clear that household suffrage was to form the basis of the actual bill: they feared that the electorates in most of the boroughs would be swamped by new working-class voters, and calculations by the government's own statisticians seemed to confirm their fears. But household

17

suffrage, *with safeguards*, was becoming increasingly popular among the Conservative rank and file in the Commons at this very time. It had the great merit of providing a popular cry, indeed of seeming to meet one of the central demands of the radical reformers, but its impact could be softened by placing legal and administrative barriers in the way of potential working-class voters, as well as by granting extra votes to the better off and better educated. Some suspected that the safeguards would be lost as the bill made its way through the Commons, but there was widespread and growing enthusiasm on the back-benches.

Those who expected the safeguards to crumble were proved right. Disraeli accepted a sequence of amendments which appeared to assure a working-class predominance in the boroughs. The bill originally envisaged household suffrage in the boroughs, limited to those who paid their rates in person rather than through their landlords, and limited also to those supposedly stable citizens who had been resident for at least two years. This was a major restriction in towns where most property was rented and there was a great deal of short-distance migration among the working class. There were to be dual votes for property-owners, and 'fancy franchises' for the thrifty and educated to counterbalance the extension of the working-class vote. The county qualification for tenants came down from £50 to £15 annual rental.

Disraeli gave up the dual votes almost immediately, and after the Easter holidays the two years' residential qualification was reduced to one, and a £10 lodger franchise in the boroughs was accepted, although it applied in practice to apartment dwellers rather than to single men in single rooms. The most controversial concession came on 17 May, when Hodgkinson's amendment to abolish compounding, the practice whereby landlords paid the rates for their tenants and thereby disfranchised them, was accepted. This proved to be disastrous for local government, but it allowed 'household suffrage' to become a reality by removing the most pervasive legal obstacle to small tenants seeking to vote. Opponents at the time argued that it would add 500,000 voters to the electorate, and the actual figure may not have been far short of that. After this the loss of the 'fancy franchises' hardly mattered.

18

The county voting qualification was also extended, most importantly by the substitution of £12 for £15 annual rental, although, significantly, this was a much less spectacular concession than had been obtained in the boroughs. One of the few proposals to come to grief was the philosopher John Stuart Mill's motion that women should be entitled to the vote on the same basis as men, as most of the House followed Mr Laird of Birkenhead, who asserted that 'although they might not be able to give a single argument for their opinion he would back their instincts against the logic of the Hon. Member'. It could be argued that the whole reform debate was a triumph of instinct over logic. Gladstone, whose thoroughly researched but utterly tedious speeches on the legal details and problems raised by the bill had been assiduously ignored by sleeping or absent colleagues, would certainly have agreed; and Disraeli's success, magnificent as it was, owed much more to cunning and versatility than to information or principle. The bill had indeed been transformed beyond recognition in its passage through the Commons. We shall look at what contemporaries thought of it, and at what its consequences were, in the next two chapters. Meanwhile, we must ask how this extraordinary event occurred.

Derby had decided to grasp the nettle of reform; but the Second Reform Act was, in the end, emphatically Disraeli's measure. It took the form it did, not because Disraeli stole the Liberals' clothing – indeed, it became apparent that the concessions he made went beyond the expectations, and even the wishes, of Bright, who expressed the fear that a 'residuum' of the unregenerate poor, too dependent and irresponsible to use the vote properly, would benefit from the measure. The Act certainly went beyond anything Gladstone might have sanctioned, although its precise form was affected by Disraeli's willingness to accept amendments from anyone other than his arch-rival. The extra-parliamentary pressure of late 1886 and early 1867 helped to create a climate of opinion in which back-bench Tory squires were willing to see their leaders pass a radical-looking measure of reform, for fear that worse might subsequently befall them. Ultimately, however, the nature of the Act was determined by the exigencies of party strife in a complex and fragmented political system, with a continuum of overlapping groups rather than a sharp divide between two well-defined parties. Disraeli's tactics were governed, once his party was committed to passing a bill of some sort, by the need to conciliate enough Whigs, Liberals and radicals to sustain his majorities, without losing the support of more than the small die-hard fringe of Conservative opponents of reform at any price. There may be something in Himmelfarb's suggestion that the Conservatives could cope with a more flexible approach to franchise reform than the Liberals, because they set more store by national identity and links between the classes, while the Liberals expected individual voters to pursue their own self-interest, narrowly and ignorantly defined, at the expense of the common good, and therefore expected the worst of new voters below their chosen level of the 'labour aristocracy'. But to argue that Disraeli had a vision of 'Tory democracy' towards which he had been 'educating' his party for years, or to suggest that he deliberately reached downwards to catch a hidden stratum of deferential working-class Tory voters, is to mistake subsequent self-justificatory rhetoric for current policy. Even his claim to be recognizing 'popular privileges', which were 'consistent with a state of society in which there is great inequality of condition', rather than 'democratic rights', which connoted equality, was not borne out by his subsequent concessions to what his opponents took to be the spirit of democracy. Above all, it is clear that Disraeli himself had no idea of the electoral consequences of the Act for which he was ultimately responsible. His was a party victory, the ultimate consequences of which could not be foreseen. Contemporaries were only too well aware of this, as their published hopes and fears reveal.

3

Reactions to the
Second Reform Act

What struck contemporaries most forcibly about the Second Reform Act was the unexpectedly wide extension of the franchise in the boroughs. As it turned out, the borough electorate in England and Wales grew by 134 per cent between 1866 and 1869, while the number of voters in the counties rose by 46 per cent and the combined total by 89 per cent. The boroughs concentrated the minds of observers at the time, and they have also concentrated the interest of most historians. But they were far from being the whole story, and opinion at the time was also affected by the redistribution of seats and alteration of boundaries which followed Reform, and by the different ways in which the rules were changed in Scotland and Ireland.

Unlike the franchise clauses of the Reform Bill, the bill for the redistribution of seats was well thought out. It was based on statistical research which had been performed with the 1866 Bill in mind. The aim was to take 30 seats from corrupt and under-populated boroughs, and give 14 to substantial new boroughs, 15 to the counties and 1 to London University. Here again, however, significant alterations were made in response to various pressures and vested interests as the bill passed through the Commons, and in the end 52 seats were redistributed from the English boroughs, 7 from towns disfranchised for corruption and 45 from boroughs with fewer than 10,000 inhabitants. Seven of these were removed from the list altogether and 35 kept only one of their previous two Members; 25 extra seats were given to the counties, and 20 to new borough constituencies. London University obtained its MP, and Merthyr Tydfil and Salford acquired a second Member each. The representation of the four largest provincial cities, Leeds, Liverpool, Manchester and Birmingham, was increased from two to three MPs apiece, but each elector retained only two votes, in the hope that the third seat would go to the minority party, which was expected to be the Conservatives. Concern to protect and advance party interest was also apparent, not only in the further increase in the county seats, but in the care which was taken to isolate rural influences, which were expected to favour the Conservatives, from the perceived Liberal and radical proclivities of the towns. This priority was expressed in the redrawing of constituency boundaries, and in the sharper segregation between the borough and county electorates which was introduced by the Second Reform Act. The ability to manipulate the system in this way was an important by-product of being the party that introduced and passed Reform, and Disraeli was well aware of the party political advantage which could be derived.

One of the key differences between the Bill of 1866 and the Act of 1867 was that the former sought to perpetuate urban influences in the county constituencies, while the latter sought to reduce them considerably. Under the rules of the First Reform Act, men who lived in boroughs and did not meet the £10 householder voting qualification were often able to vote in the county; and in heavily urbanized counties this meant that large numbers of urban shopkeeepers and artisans were able to dilute the influence of the landowners and, it was believed, swell the anti-Conservative vote. The Second Reform Act ended this state of affairs, except in the smaller market towns which were not parliamentary boroughs, because it provided a vote in the borough for the urban householders who had previously augmented the county electorate, and prevented them from continuing to vote in the county. The idea was to abandon most of the boroughs to the Liberals and radicals while making the county seats safe for the Conservatives. To assist the process still further, Disraeli tried to manage the commission which revised the constituency boundaries, so as to extend the boundaries of the boroughs to include suburbs and outlying industrial villages, and mop up as many bodies of politically suspect voters as possible. The commission was packed with Conservative country gentlemen, and proposed enormous expansions of borough boundaries. Eighty-one boroughs were to be extended, five to include populations of over 400,000 each while the adjacent county divisions had less than 100,000. These extreme proposals were torpedoed in the Commons, and the extensions to fifteen of the largest boroughs were severely pruned; but D. C. Moore argues that nevertheless much of the strategy remained intact. The redistribution of seats certainly perpetuated existing constitutional imbalances within England and Wales, with the rural south and west keeping a disproportionate number of seats compared with London and the North and Midlands; and the counties had increased their number of MPs at the expense of the boroughs. The knowledge that this would be the outcome of a Conservative Reform Act may well have made Disraeli and his allies less fearful of the possible consequences of expanding the borough electorate.

Redistribution and boundary changes were completed by June 1868; and by this time the promised Reform Acts for Scotland and Ireland had also been delivered. Scotland acquired seven extra seats, which were taken from small English boroughs. There was no lodger franchise as in England, but F. B. Smith points out that 'Lodgers had qualified in Scotland since 1832 because there they were legally tenants' (1966, 226). Otherwise, it was the mixture as in England, with most of the conflict arising from the relationship between county and borough. Ireland, as usual, was different. The key reform here had been the Irish Franchise Act of 1850, which brought order to a chaotic system and more than trebled the Irish electorate. By contrast, the Act of 1868 has been described as 'extremely mouse-like': it 'left the important county franchise quite alone and merely reduced the valuation required for the borough vote from eight pounds to over four pounds' (Hoppen 1985, 215). The proportion of Irish adult males with the vote fell far behind that for the rest of Britain.

After 1868 as before, Ireland accounted for 105 of the 658 parliamentary seats; so the very limited, almost negligible, impact of reform here is important and should be borne in mind. Scotland's representation went up from 53 to 60, that of England fell from 471 to 464, and that of Wales remained at 29. The balance between county and borough seats tilted towards the former, from 253:399 to 280:369 (the University seats accounted for the rest). In England the change was particularly marked, from 144:323 to 169:290. As with the franchise provisions and boundary changes, this was intended to make the political world safer for the influence of rural landowners and, usually, for the Conservative Party. Moreover, even after reform and redistribution, 'The old world of quiet medieval market towns like Calne, Eye and Bridgnorth, or Coleraine and Armagh . . . continued until 1885 to return more than half the borough members and more than one-fifth of the House of Commons', according to Professor Hanham's calculations (1959, 39). Many of the smaller boroughs were strongly influenced or even effectively controlled by local landowners, and the fifty-four English boroughs with populations of less than 10,000 were predominantly Tory in 1868 and 1874. Again, it is well worth remembering that not all boroughs were large and dynamic manufacturing towns; and the carefully calculated survival of the small boroughs, open as they were to traditional influences, provides a further explanation for the acceptability of Disraeli's Reform Act to many Conservatives.

For whatever reasons, Disraeli and Derby carried their party with them, and with surprisingly few immediate misgivings. Cowling is no doubt correct to suggest that 'There was nothing inevitable about the course they followed. If a restrictive Act could have been passed on a conservative basis, they would have passed it' (1967, 308). As it was,

Even if Disraeli foresaw the outcome, Derby almost certainly did not, had no intention of conceding to popular agitation or the parliamentary Radicals, and was led on, like everyone else in the Conservative party, because he convinced himself that no measure that was in sight would make much difference to the social structure and wanted to win more than he wanted anything else.   (p. 310)

The only query here concerns the degree of unanimity in the Conservative Party at large.

The banker, economist and constitutional theorist Walter Bagehot is worth quoting at length on this issue.

> Generally, the debates upon the passing of an Act contain much valuable instruction as to what may be expected of it. But the debates on the Reform Bill of 1867 hardly tell anything. They are taken up with technicalities as to the ratepayers and the compound householder. Nobody in the country knew what was being done. I happened at the time to visit a purely agricultural and conservative county, and I asked the local Tories, 'Do you understand this Reform Bill? Do you know that your Conservative government has brought in a Bill far more Radical than any former Bill, and that it is very likely to be passed?' The answer I got was, 'What stuff you talk! How can it be a Radical Reform Bill? Why, *Bright* opposes it!' There was no answering that in a way which a 'common jury' could understand. The Bill was supported by the *The Times* and opposed by Mr Bright; and therefore the mass of Conservatives and of common moderate people without distinction of party, had no conception of the effect. They said it was 'London nonsense' if you tried to explain it to them.   (1872, xvi)

We shall see that Bagehot had worries of his own about where the Second Reform Act was taking the constitution. He was conscious that he was not alone:

> Many, perhaps most, of the intelligent Conservatives were fearful of the consequences of the proposal; but as it was made by the heads of their own party, they did not like to oppose it, and the discipline of party carried them with it.   (p. xvii)

This contemporary testimony provides a different emphasis from Cowling's interpretation; and not 'everyone' in the Conservative Party endorsed this measure of reform. Some Tories were openly antagonistic at the time. Robert Cecil, Viscount Cranborne, one of the trio of resigners from the Cabinet on 2 March 1867, attacked the Second Reform Bill in parliament and in that august periodical, the *Quarterly Review*. He feared that a democratic Britain would come to be governed on a spoils system by trade union leaders and corrupt professional party managers, purporting to govern in the interests of the working classes rather than those of the nation at large, but really soaking the rich and ruining the country. More practically, he suspected that household suffrage in the smaller boroughs would loosen the Conservatives' hold on them, and bring electoral disaster in the short run as well as national calamity over a long period. The fear of socialism and of working-class dominance of the constitution was widely shared among Conservatives, and quickly came to the surface when the immediate euphoria of parliamentary victory had died away. The Liberal general election victory under the new rules in 1868 reinforced the less apocalyptic of these fears. Paul Smith suggests that 'the great bulk of the party had never desired Reform, and resented the way in which Disraeli led them into a measure of such size' (1967, 92). Many of the country gentlemen, still the backbone of the party's support in the Commons, came to feel betrayed, and analogies were even drawn with Peel's repeal of the Corn Laws in 1846, which had split the Conservatives so damagingly. Suggestions that the new urban working-class voters would be deferential and amenable to influence from above were not yet widely believed, especially among landowners who were unwilling to broaden the Conservatives' social base beyond the agricultural countryside. Cranborne's frame of mind had always been influential among traditionalists in the party, and after the 1868 election his unease became more widely propagated. He and Disraeli remained at loggerheads, and there was considerable support for his political promotion to the Leadership of the House of Lords after his succession as Marquis of Salisbury. This would have made Disraeli's position untenable, and for some time there was a serious threat to his leadership of the party, fuelled partly by the growing opposition among Conservatives to the electoral consequences and presumed long-term implications of the 1867 Act. Much of Disraeli's support had been fickle, ill-informed or blindly partisan, and there were many second thoughts and reservations in the aftermath of the Act.

The more famously expressed fears, of course, were those on the Liberal side. Bagehot himself stood for parliament in Liberal guise at Bridgwater in 1866, although Norman St John-Stevas suggests that 'there was little to distinguish him from a progressive and open-minded Conservative . . . his natural scepticism and his vein of cynicism inclined him towards Conservatism, while his intellect made him a moderate Liberal' (1959, 18). His affinity with a conservative world-view was based on 'deep feeling and reverence for the past' (p. 45), for custom and tradition. It is no surprise to find a deep distrust of radical parliamentary reform in his writings, and especially in the classic work for which he is remembered, *The English Constitution*. In the first edition of this very important book, two years before the Second Reform Act, Bagehot expressed his fears of the consequences of the 'ultra-democratic theory' of reform, whereby 'every man of twenty-one years of age (if not every woman too) should have an equal vote in electing Parliament', with equal electoral districts. He thought that this would lead to the Commons being dominated by 'an unmixed squirearchy' from the countryside, and a mixture of 'the genuine representatives of the [urban] artizans' and 'the merely pretended members for [the common order of workpeople] whom I may call the members for the public-houses'. Rural paternalism and urban corruption would combine to produce a deeply-divided Commons composed of mutually irreconcilable extremists. Bagehot accepted that a moderate measure of reform should give the intelligent artisans a distinct voice of their own in urban constituencies with a wide franchise, but he feared any extension of democracy on a broader front.

The Second Reform Act went far enough to arouse Bagehot's severest misgivings, and he voiced them in the introduction to the second edition of his book, published in 1872. He expected that the enfranchisement of ignorant unskilled labourers would undermine or outflank 'the deference of the old electors to their betters [which] was the only way in which our old system could be maintained'; and he worried that when the new electorate learned its potential power and strength, the political parties might be tempted to 'bid for the support of the working man', offering concessions and raising questions which threatened property and political stability. Statesmen, he argued, must be particularly careful not to raise and agitate questions which tended to unite the working classes against their 'betters'; the agenda of politics must be so drawn up as to avoid any such socially dangerous issues.

Bagehot was not the only right-wing Liberal to be haunted by the spectre of class politics and the 'supremacy of ignorance over instruction and of numbers over knowledge'. The Adullamites, with Robert Lowe as their most vituperative spokesman, had expressed just these concerns during the reform debates of 1866 and 1867. Lowe saw no reason to reform an electoral system which was already, as he saw it, providing good government. He denied that any individual had a natural or God-given right to the vote, and put the efficient protection of property and order ahead of any notion of a moral right to active participation in the constitution. He went much further than Bagehot in his strictures on the working class in politics, posing the famous question in a speech on the 1866 Reform Bill,

> If you want venality, if you want ignorance, if you want drunkenness and the facility for being intimidated, or if . . . you want impulsive unreflecting and violent people, where do you look for them in constituencies? Do you go to the top or the bottom?

He alleged that democracy would inevitably degenerate into mob rule, dominated by corrupt career politicians; and he claimed that this situation already prevailed in Australia and the United States, while historically the Greek and Roman experience of democracy suggested that it led inexorably to tyranny and moral degeneration. Working-class voters would pursue their own, narrowly-defined self-interest, and would lack the education and sense of responsibility to look to the interests of society as a whole. Moreover, they would promote trade union interests, give additional power to central government to intervene on their behalf, and obstruct the free play of competition and market forces which was held to be the basis for mid-Victorian prosperity. This was the angriest and most sustained critique of reform, and it attracted much support from Liberal believers in free trade and minimum government intervention. It also roused the unforgiving anger of working-class political activists and their spokesmen, and Lowe's insulting words came back to haunt him in speech after speech.

Many other Liberals were at best ambivalent about radical reform, but they were much more tentative in their ideas and less outspoken in their expression. Gladstone himself, despite the ambiguities of some of his past rhetoric, made his position clear in a published letter on 8 August 1866: 'I do not agree with the demand either for manhood or for household suffrage: while I own with regret that the conduct of the opponents of the Government measure of this year has done much to encourage that demand.' Throughout the reform campaign of 1867 he remained anxious to exclude the occupants of the cheapest housing from the widened franchise. Even John Bright, though he was perceived as a dangerous agitator and demagogue by a large proportion of the political nation, began to equivocate when household suffrage began to appear a real possibility rather than a basis for negotiation, in the early months of 1867; and Bagehot was cruel but not entirely misleading when he commented sardonically on the radical dilemma a few years later:

Many Radical members who had been asking for years for household suffrage were much more surprised than pleased at the near chance of obtaining it; they had asked for it as bargainers ask for the highest possible price, but they never expected to get it. Altogether the Liberals, or at least the extreme Liberals, were much like a man who has been pushing hard against an opposing door, till, on a sudden, the door opens, the resistance ceases, and he is thrown violently forward.

(pp. xvii–xviii)

Bright had invested too much in radical reform over the years to repudiate the achievement of household suffrage, whatever his forebodings about the 'residuum' might be; and one biographer tells us that he was 'overjoyed' at the passing of the Act, despite his revulsion at the Conservatives' 'opportunism and hypocrisy'. But fears about the possible consequences of the Act were less easily suspended or set aside in other influential quarters, and they were given added encouragement by the pronouncements of popular

29

intellectuals and opinion-formers. Thomas Carlyle's blusteringly incoherent apocalyptic vision saw reform as 'shooting Niagara', part of England's headlong rush to the bottomless pit of democracy, 'The calling in of new supplies of blockheadism, gullibility, bribability, amenability to beer and balderdash, by way of amending the woes we have had from our previous supplies of that bad article'. Carlyle yearned for a reassertion of virtuous, aristocratic authority; and fears of the potential consequences of working-class electoral predominance were also expressed by the poet, school inspector and standard-bearer of 'culture', Matthew Arnold. He, too, discerned a tendency to anarchy in the political developments of the time, and responded angrily to the Hyde Park 'riots', suggesting that authority was losing its vigour and self-confidence in the face of a growing propensity to 'rowdyism' on the part of a working class which was becoming as assertive as its betters in the defence of its rights. John Ruskin, the great art historian and social prophet, was also sceptical about the trend to democracy, which he

> once saw finely illustrated by the beetles of North Switzerland, who by universal suffrage . . . one May twilight, carried it that they would fly over the Lake of Zug; and flew short, to the great disfigurement of the Lake of Zug . . . and to the close of the cockchafer democracy for that year. (1907, 280)

Ruskin's choice of example expressed the social distance that many of the educated classes felt from the newly enfranchised.

Ultimately, perhaps, although their prescriptions for social improvement differed, Ruskin, Arnold, Carlyle and Bagehot all preferred a stable, hierarchical society, in which the rulers were men of property who recognized that they had duties and responsibilities towards their social inferiors as well as rights over them. They were suspicious of the turmoil and threat to order associated with democracy, and at bottom they identified with the rule of an idealized aristocracy of breeding, *noblesse oblige*, culture and intellect. In this they were representative of the educated orthodoxies of the day, however heretical Ruskin and Arnold, in particular, might be on other matters. There were other well-publicized intellectual viewpoints, however, which presented the

Reform Act of 1867 in a more favourable light. The political philosopher John Stuart Mill, whose ideas commanded wide respect among the Liberals and who was MP for the predominantly working-class constituency of Westminster when the Second Reform Act went through Parliament, was a guarded but genuine supporter of reform. But he was acutely concerned to protect the rights of minorities, and would have preferred special arrangements to ensure that room was found in parliament for dissident intellectuals, and he suspected that a working-class electorate might ultimately pursue legislation to advance its own class interest, while fearing that a democratically elected parliament would be short on legal and administrative efficiency.

More positively still, an impressive collection of mainly Oxbridge academics could be assembled in 1867, after the defeat of the Liberal Reform Bill, to expose the contradictions in Lowe's anti-reform arguments and to celebrate the political virtues and sagacity of the organized working class. Christopher Kent suggests that they hoped to benefit from 'a more rational variety of deference – intellectual rather than feudal', giving more power to disinterested reasoning and undermining the tyranny of vested interests. Here were would-be opinion-formers who did not fear working-class enfranchisement, and indeed embraced it warmly; and there were university men, lawyers and journalists, among the activist organizers of meetings and demonstrations during 1866–7. Professor Beesly, in particular, became a bogeyman of similar proportions to John Bright among the opponents of reform. Also prominent among these supporters of an extensive measure of reform was Frederic Harrison, an Oxford-educated barrister and journalist, and disciple of the French philosopher Auguste Comte. Scathing as he was about the limited political vision of the pre-Reform electorate, with its preponderance of petty tradesmen and penny-pinching shopkeepers, and optimistic as he was about the working-class capacity to bring the pressure of principled public opinion to bear in healthy ways, Harrison was reassuring about the extent of the threat to the social order that the Second Reform Act posed. He argued that

Wealth and its public influence will always be felt in any society. . . . How much more in a social system so complex and well knit as ours? Every one who has looked attentively into the prospects of at least the forthcoming elections sees how very strong wealth and rank are certain to prove . . . the bulk of the men who sit in [the House of Commons] will be the same hearty and sensible gentlemen who now give the tone to that distinguished Club. (1975, 167)

Here was an assessment to warm Bagehot's heart, and it came from one of the most radical of the really articulate commentators on reform. But how far could this comfortably-off intellectual speak for the mass of trade unionists and working-class reformers? More to the point, how far could he assess the political outlook and voting behaviour of those who had not campaigned for the vote, but were about to be offered the franchise for the first time? This leads us to the central question: how did the Second Reform Act work out in practice? Who gained the vote, and how did they use it? What political changes can be attributed to its passing? And which of the contemporary commentators came nearest to predicting the actual outcome?

4

The impact of reform

Reactions to the Second Reform Act were influenced above all by the expectations and fears of contemporary commentators about the number and nature of the new voters, especially in the towns. Impressive as it was, the rise in the number of borough voters was less than it might have been. The one-year residential qualification reduced the number of potential voters considerably, although it came to be interpreted in a more relaxed way which allowed householders moving *within* a borough to retain their vote. Pauperism disqualified many, and was to do so for years to come; and in many towns it proved impossible to abolish compounding, as tenants refused to pay their rates in person and arrears of collection mounted rapidly in the late 1860s. The persistence of compounding, which had to be tolerated because of the sheer scale on which it took place, led to anomalies; in some boroughs compounders were allowed on to the electoral register in 1868, but in others they were excluded. In 1869, Gladstone's government resolved the issue by quietly enacting that compounders should be allowed to vote on the same basis as those who paid their rates in person. As Seymour remarks, this amounted to the settling without controversy in 1869 of an issue that had generated agonized debate two years previously; it was 'the removal of the last great restriction upon pure household suffrage'.

The problem of the compounders helped to ensure that the number of new borough voters was significantly less in 1868 than in 1874, and that the experience of different constituencies varied widely. The status of miners in rent-free colliery houses remained anomalous even after 1869, and it is significant that, when, after a campaign, miners in Morpeth, Northumberland, were allowed in 1873 to vote as if they were compound householders, the local electorate increased immediately from 2600 to 4900. This led to the election in 1874 of the miners' leader Thomas Burt as one of the first pair of working-class MPs. This is, among other things, a reminder that some of the changes brought about under the Second Reform Act required several years, and additional legislation, before they came to fruition.

What really counted, however, was not so much the holding of a theoretical right to vote as the recognition of that right by the compilers of the electoral register. Even in the immediate aftermath of the First Reform Act, the political parties soon learnt that, as Derek Fraser puts it, 'there was only one qualification to vote, namely actually to be on the register'. By the late 1860s most urban constituencies, at least, had a cohort of activists from both the established parties, who devoted their time and accumulated expertise to the protection of voting rights for the supporters of their party, and sought the removal of opponents, or even of people whose politics were doubtful, from the register. It had long been clear that elections could be won or lost on this basis alone. The registers themselves were often incompetently prepared under the careless supervision of unpaid overseers of the poor, and there was plenty of scope for challenging the voting rights of people whose address might have been wrongly recorded or whose status as householder might be open to dispute. In some constituencies thousands of objections were made each year by party organizers, as a matter of regular routine, in an attempt to reduce the numbers of their actual or potential opponents as far as possible. Without the protection of a party machine, a would-be voter was often helpless against this kind of manoeuvring. The hearings which determined disputed voting rights were held during working hours, no compensation was paid for loss of time, and few of the victims could afford legal representation. Lodgers, who had to make out a case for their inclusion on the register, had a particularly hard time. As Gladstone had predicted in 1866, too much time and trouble were involved for most working-class lodgers to be able to qualify. As a result, the number of lodgers acquiring the vote was so small as to be politically negligible. Seymour tells us that

> In the [London] boroughs the number of lodgers was estimated at between two and three hundred thousand; but the number on the electoral register in 1868 was only about fourteen thousand. Apparently the difficulties were so great that most of the few who were registered became discouraged, for in 1872 there were only four thousand registered lodgers in the entire metropolis . . . and . . . in 1872, outside of London, there were only five thousand lodger voters in all of England and Wales.   (1970, 364)

Very few lodgers were able to obtain the vote unless they had the backing of a political party, and the strong tendency was for working-class voters in general to be drawn from those with clear and well-known partisan political attachments. This may help to explain the very high percentage turn-outs in so many mid-Victorian elections; those who were able to secure and safeguard their place on the electoral register were also disproportionately likely to be politically committed to one or other of the established parties. This state of affairs also helps to explain the failure of separate working-class political organizations to emerge: it was a practical way in which the dice were loaded against them, for it cost a great deal of money to work the registration system in this way.

Despite these obstacles, the number of urban working-class voters did increase enormously in the aftermath of the Second Reform Act. On the eve of Reform, and on a generous definition, a parliamentary return found that in 1865 'working-class' voters accounted for anything between 7 per cent of the electorate (in Leeds) and 40 per cent (in Leicester). The 1867 Act, however, brought substantial working-class majorities to the electoral registers of almost all the boroughs. The changes were most marked in specialized industrial towns: the number of voters increased more than tenfold in Merthyr Tydfil, sixfold in Oldham and South Shields, fivefold in Halifax, Stoke, Blackburn and Bolton, fourfold in Leeds and threefold in Birmingham. Older boroughs gained less remarkably: in Liverpool the increase was 90 per cent, in the London boroughs it was two-thirds, and in small-town constituencies like Hertford and Weymouth it might be only 40 per cent. The advent of household suffrage was only part of the explanation for these increases. In many places there were boundary extensions, and as the new franchises were added to the existing ones, rather than replacing them, the voting lists in towns where compounding had been widely practised, such as Brighton, included many additional £10 householders who had previously been denied the vote. Lodgers, as we have seen, were generally unimportant: at their most numerous, in Westminster, they never formed more than 10 per cent of any local electorate. Interestingly, the so-called 'ancient right' voters were more numerous than the lodgers, and this remained the case into the 1880s: the surviving holders of a variety of peculiar, local, pre-1832 voting rights accounted for at least 10 per cent of the electorate in twenty-eight post-1867 boroughs, and in nine they were more than a quarter of the voters.

The variations in the growth of borough electorates arose partly because the old £10 householder and 'ancient right' franchises had given the vote to far more people in some places than in others. The impact of the Second Reform Act in this respect was much greater in towns where small houses, cheap rents, compounding, or lax assessment for rates had kept the number of £10 householders on the voting lists relatively low. Indeed, the more genuinely uniform franchise of 1867 tended to iron out the differences between boroughs, although its effect took time to become apparent. On average, one in seven of the borough population had the vote after 1867, although the London boroughs lagged behind some of the manufacturing towns in this respect. The counties gained far fewer voters, of course, and here the post-1867 ratio was one in fourteen. The difference between the county and borough franchises was now the cause of visible and glaring anomalies, with people living in identical houses having the vote if they lived on the borough side of a boundary road, but being left out in the cold if they lived on the county side. The resulting protests and arguments would help to ensure the further extension of the county franchise in 1884.

Even so, this was a much more democratic electoral system than hitherto. What difference did it make to voting patterns and party politics? The organized working class had celebrated the coming of Reform with rallies, processions and banners. How did they use their votes?

The most obvious introductory point here is that the established parties continued to hold sway. At first, the optimistic expectations of the reformist elements amongst the Liberals seemed justified, for the first post-Reform general election brought them into power with an overwhelming majority. Evans calculates that Gladstone's government could expect the support of 387 MPs, compared with the Conservatives' 271. Bagehot was sceptical about the long-term implications of this result:

> The circumstances were too exceptional. In the first place, Mr Gladstone's personal popularity was such as has not been seen since the time of Mr Pitt, and such as may never be seen again. . . . The remains, too, of the old electoral organisation were exceedingly powerful; the old voters voted as they had been told, and the new voters mostly voted with them. . . . At the last election, the trial of the new system hardly began, and, as far as it did begin, it was favoured by a peculiar guidance.
>
> (pp. xviii–xix)

Bagehot knew little or nothing about how or why working-class people voted, and when the 1874 election confirmed his doubts about the permanency of Liberal dominance, it did so by bringing in a Conservative government with a comfortable majority and a very considerable body of urban working-class support. The pendulum was to swing back again in 1880, but the advent of the first clear-cut Conservative majority in the Commons since Peel's time gave contemporaries cause for surprise and speculation. Few were able to say, with Frederic Harrison, that they had predicted this outcome. But the 1868 election had provided interesting hints of widespread working-class Conservative support, and we should examine this phenomenon a little more closely.

The general election of 1868 has been much studied by historians at constituency level. This was a unique parliamentary general election in that it combined open voting with the widened electoral franchise of 1867. Where poll-books have survived, listing individual voters and recording the ways in which they cast their votes, it has been possible to analyse voting patterns in detail. Sometimes, voters' occupations or addresses are listed in the poll-books, or can be traced (tediously and often uncertainly) in other sources. It is even possible in some constituencies, as Nossiter's work shows for an earlier period, to find out the rateable value of voters' houses, their ages, and how many servants they kept, by cross-referring to rate-books and the manuscript census returns. Much can be learnt from this about what sort of people voted for what sort of candidates, although there are many pitfalls. Above all, even when we can say who people voted for, we hardly ever have any hard evidence on *why* they chose to vote that way. Was it because they believed in the declared policies of a particular party? Was it because they respected and deferred to a particular candidate, or an influential local figure, a nobleman or big industrialist, who supported him? Was it because they feared eviction, dismissal or loss of trade if they voted against the wishes of their landlord, employer or best customers? Was it because they had been bribed, or were afraid of violence being directed against them if they voted the 'wrong' way in the eyes of their neighbours or 'betters'? Some of these considerations were more important to some people than to others, and some bulked larger in some constituencies than in others.

Perhaps the most clear-cut conclusion to emerge from the poll-book studies is that voters' preference did not divide in any visibly systematic way along class lines. Voting cut across occupational divisions rather than reflecting or expressing them, and the same applies to the more important, but less accessible, distinctions between employers, self-employed and employees, who might often share the same occupational label (such as 'shoemaker') in our sources. The corollary of this, of course, is that there were significant numbers not only of Liberal-voting property-owners and employers, which should occasion no surprise, but also of Conservative-voting working men. A few specific occupational groups (publicans voting Conservative when faced with Liberal candidates of the temperance persuasion, Church of England clergy voting Conservative for fear of legislation directed against the Church's privileges promoted by the Nonconformists in the Liberal Party) voted pretty solidly one way or the other, but this was exceptional. An unknown number of individuals may have cast their votes out of partly or wholly class-related motives (perhaps especially where trade union loyalties were at issue), but fears that the wider franchise in the boroughs would bring about a general pattern of class-based voting were not borne out in 1868, or for long afterwards. Indeed, there is considerable doubt as to whether such a pattern has ever predominated, even in twentieth-century Britain.

After 1867, as before, class divisions as such were far from being central to voting behaviour. This is not surprising, as there was no specifically working-class party, while the Conservatives were no longer identified solely with the interests of agriculture and the landed gentry. Both the established parties were competing at constituency level in the boroughs for the new working-class vote. But what induced members of the new electorate to cast their votes for one side or the other (when their choice, of course, was limited by the parties' choice of candidate)? Can we identify the rise of new influences on voting, and perhaps the decline of older ones, in the expanded post-1867 urban electorates?

The small amount of poll-book evidence we have on how individuals voted at successive elections suggests that most were party loyalists rather than floating voters, and we have seen that the registration process was likely to produce a predominantly committed electorate. So long-term influences involving such basic aspects of life as employment, religion, schooling, neighbourhood, club membership and even drinking place were more likely to have a strong impact on voting behaviour than were the issues raised and brandished during particular election campaigns. Speeches and rallies were probably designed more to rally the faithful than to generate converts. Party policy and presentation had to match the expectations of supporters, but allegiance was more a matter of long-term socialization than of informed judgement. Where issues did make a difference, local matters remained at least as important as national policies for many years after 1867. Questions of local government, local office-holding, rates, schools and charities often dominated discussion, with the 'official' issues relegated to the background. Candidates were expected to be aware of local concerns and willing to defend local interests in parliament, easing the path of legislation which would benefit the constituency. Extensive donations to local charities were expected, and the relative generosity of the rival candidates often became a matter of public dispute. These expectations favoured local employers or wealthy outsiders, and it is not surprising that, to use Nossiter's words, 'influence' remained more important than 'opinion'. The well-informed, independent-minded working-class voter, of whom reformers had expected so much, remained a rarity. Indeed, blunter instruments of immediate persuasion, in the form of coercion, intimidation and bribery, survived the Second Reform Act and even, in some places, outlasted the introduction of the secret ballot in 1872.

Patrick Joyce has suggested that in the textile factory towns of Lancashire and Yorkshire, and perhaps elsewhere, the owners of the larger mills were able to command the political loyalty of their work-forces, just as rural landowners were able to secure the votes of their tenants for the candidates of their choice. Thus in Blackburn the inhabitants of the streets surrounding mills with Liberal owners voted overwhelmingly Liberal, while similar patterns of Conservative support surrounded Tory factories. Joyce explains such phenomena in terms of the authority of the head of the family firm, as a father-figure to his workpeople, who shared in his celebrations and identified their interests with his. This authority was delegated through the supervisory workers, and spread outwards into the community surrounding the factory, where the employer's control over housing and his patronage of churches, schools and other institutions extended his dominance still further. So the identification of the individual voter with employer, workplace and community placed him in a web of dependence and loyalty from which it was almost impossible to escape. On this argument, then, the popular politics of the industrial north after 1867 was dominated by a 'new feudalism' of control by the large employers.

This explanation for the vitality of established party politics in the boroughs after 1867 has not gone unchallenged. Most adult men, even in the 'cotton towns', worked outside the cotton factories, although employers in other industries such as engineering might also have had pretensions to political influence over their work-forces, and some of the railway companies certainly did. Many factories, accounting for a substantial minority of the workpeople, were much smaller than Joyce's version of the large paternalist firm would suggest; and outside the industrial heartland, small concerns remained the norm. Although some, like the gas company or the builder Charles Parsons in Lewes (Sussex) in 1868, might have suspiciously unanimous work-forces at election time, their overall importance to popular politics can have been only marginal. Employer housing was much less prevalent than Joyce suggests, and a more recent study of the Blackburn firm of Harrisons shows that substantial numbers of employees might live a quarter of a mile or more from the workplace, while nearly 40 per cent of the voters employed by this strongly partisan Tory firm failed to vote the mill-owner's way. Joyce's own figures always show minorities of dissidents even in the most partisan streets, and Blackburn, which provides a lot of the evidence for his argument, was unusual in its large number of clearly defined mill-centred communities. Elsewhere, the pattern of voting for which he argues is harder to demonstrate, as recent studies of Stockport and Bradford confirm, while in Preston most workers appeared, if anything, to be voting against the wishes of their employers, in an inversion of Joyce's expectations.

Even if we could show more convincingly that most workers voted the same way as their boss, we would still be left wondering why this happened. Joyce presents us, ultimately, with a deferential working class, whose members accepted that their employer knew best and had their political interests at heart. As he admits, however, this is not the whole story. Working-class voters might have identified more with the mill or the neighbourhood than with the employer, and in a period when the outcome of an election was visibly unlikely to make any serious difference to their lives, they could afford to indulge in political partisanship for its own sake, akin to the support for football teams that was soon to become a consuming passion. There was endemic conflict over wages, hours and conditions between masters and men in most

41

industries, too, which casts doubt on the reality or depth of urban political deference. There is clear evidence of coercion at the Blackburn election of 1868, and in many other cases, as the 'screw' was put on and sackings and evictions were threatened and indeed, carried out. Even where some employees did decide to vote with their employers, the decision must often have been a matter of sullen or passive acquiescence rather than enthusiastic commitment.

In addition, as Dutton and King have pointed out, the employers' scope for extending their control beyond the work-place was really very limited, except in a few cases where auto-cratic mill-owners sought to supervise everything from drinking habits to washing day and sleeping arrangements. At most, there were occasional treats and excursions, and a measure of involve-ment in schools, churches, charities and benefit societies, which still left a great deal of autonomy for all but the most determinedly sycophantic. To account effectively for the voting behaviour of the new electors, we must take into account other social influences which sometimes came partially within the orbit of the factory, but which had for the vast majority an independent existence of their own. At their strongest, the arguments for the overriding political importance of the employer and the workplace provide only a partial explanation for the assimilation of the new working-class voters into the existing system, and for the appearance of so many working-class Conservatives. Even in Blackburn, other factors must be considered; and in London, or the complex and idiosyncratic large-town economies of Leeds, Liverpool or Birmingham, or the smaller market towns with their expanded semi-rural boundaries, they must have completely over-shadowed the separate political influence of the employer as such.

The central importance of the relationship between religious divisions and political allegiance persisted after 1867, though not quite as before. Some of the new voters were Nonconformists, but in general Protestant Nonconformity drew its active sup-porters from rather higher in the social scale. The important strand of Nonconformist Liberalism, which both strengthened and divided the party, was probably weakened in the boroughs by an overwhelming majority of the uncommitted or (from various perspectives) the hostile in the post-1867 electorate. The chapel-going tradesmen and artisans, previously numerically important among the voters, were swamped by working-class abstainers from organized religion, although of course there was a varying leavening of committed supporters both of the Church of England and of the Roman Catholics. Religious issues were, however, very important in the 1868 election. The Liberal proposal to dis-establish the Irish branch of the Church of England was widely seen as a threat to the special position of the Church of England itself, and, worse still, it gave aid and comfort to the Roman Catholic Church and 'Popery', assisting the Vatican's plans for a spiritual and political reconquest of the United Kingdom. There were emotive issues here, and politicians, clergymen and dema-gogues were able to use them to stir up a remarkable amount of passionate working-class support for the Conservatives. This went far beyond the small working-class church-going population, although it could call on residual loyalties drawn from school and Sunday school attendance under Church of England auspices. It was partly a matter of patriotic traditionalism, a defence of Church and constitution out of blind loyalty and fear of change and foreigners – a popular frame of mind which was already well established during the tempestuous 1790s, and had never dis-appeared. But it also fed on working-class hostility to Roman Catholic Irish migrants, especially in the larger towns, where ethnic hostility had been fuelled by a supposed Irish threat to the jobs and wages of the locals, and by identification of the Irish with a subculture of crime and violence. So disestablishment of the Irish Church was more than just a religious issue, and it engaged working-class passions in urban constituencies from Lewes to Salford. Popular anti-Catholicism was a potent electoral force after the Second Reform Act, and although it was never again as prominent as in 1868 (except in Liverpool, where sectarian con-flict was endemic), we should note that the electoral passions of the new working-class voters were more readily aroused by religious issues which cut across class lines, than by the economic issues which might have pitted one class against another.

The absence almost everywhere of class-related issues from the 1868 election campaign, and the failure of organized labour to

43

make an effective political impact, were in large part due to the successful hijacking of the Reform League by the Liberal Party. As Royden Harrison argues, the Reform League was the likeliest vehicle for a working-class assault on the reformed parliament. In July 1867 it had 600 branches and 65,000 members, widely spread throughout the United Kingdom. Many of its supporters were eager to see working-class candidates elected, and especially those who would safeguard the position of trade unions, which was currently under threat. But the League was short of money, and the enlarged electorate made election organization even more expensive than hitherto. So its political activity was dependent on largesse from middle-class Liberals of means, especially the textile manufacturer Samuel Morley. The League's secretary, George Howell, an ambitious former bricklayer who hoped to get into parliament himself, was at bottom an orthodox Gladstonian Liberal who saw no need for a wider working-class representation. He took care to distance the League's leadership from potentially embarrassing pronouncements in support of Fenian terrorists in Ireland, and negotiated with Liberal manufacturers and the Liberal whips to provide research and mediation between warring Liberal factions in key constituencies. The idea was to prevent the Liberals' chances from being compromised by the appearance of rival candidates from the Whig and working-class wings of the party, though there were many shades of grey in between. In practice, despite the League's ostensible political credentials, its influence (and its paymasters' money) was consistently used to deter radical and working-class candidates from coming forward if there was any possibility of their threatening an established MP or mainstream candidate. The pliability of the League's leadership astonished the Liberal managers, and no concessions were sought in return for the organization's help. Thus, for example, the miners' leader Alexander Macdonald was eased out of the Liberal candidature at Kilmarnock, to be replaced with Howell's enthusiastic support by (of all people) Edwin Chadwick, the principal architect of the widely hated New Poor Law of 1834. In the end the only working-class candidates actually put forward under the auspices of the Reform League were Howell himself and the carpenter W. R. Cremer, in the 'hopeless' seats of Aylesbury and Warwick. The first working-class MPs did not appear until 1874, and even then they were tied to the coat-tails of the Liberal Party.

So organized labour, deprived of leadership, cash and issues, made no effective showing in 1868, and despite the coming of the secret ballot it did little better thereafter. The trade unions themselves were still dominated by the 'labour aristocracies' of craftsmen and supervisory workers, and preferred to bring pressure and argument to bear on the established parties rather than set up a separate political organization of their own. The Liberals had effectively taken over the institutions of organized labour, in so far as they had a parliamentary political dimension, while the Conservatives made inroads among the rank and file. No doubt they were helped by the passing of the Liberals' Criminal Law Amendment Act in 1871, which turned out to make peaceful picketing in strikes illegal, and aroused widespread working-class resentment and protest. But quite apart from the political weakness of the labour movement, the formation of a separate Labour Party with its own programme, which was regularly advocated by intellectuals of the left such as Beesly, was pre-empted by the rapid establishment of a network of working men's Liberal and Conservative Clubs at constituency and ward level. These played a crucial part in attaching the new voters to the established parties.

The late 1860s saw a great expansion in the number of local Conservative Clubs, and a high proportion of their membership seems to have been working-class, especially in Lancashire. The National Union of Conservative and Constitutional Associations was founded in 1867, and under John Gorst the relationship between the central party machine and the localities was articulated and lubricated, although some of the party's aristocrats were suspicious of this populist trend and the organization was allowed to slide after the 1874 election victory. The Liberals were slightly slower into the field, and they suffered from inhibitions about allowing drink and billiards into their clubs, which made it more difficult for them to reach out to the apathetic masses of the working-class. But the Birmingham model of a so-called 'caucus' system based on popular mobilization at ward level gained ground during the 1870s. This was a direct response to a peculiar feature of the Second Reform Act, the appearance of big-city three-member constituencies in which each elector only had two votes. In Birmingham, a Liberal stronghold, it seemed that with careful organization, the Liberal vote could be evenly split between three candidates in such a way that they would all be elected. So it proved, although electoral success was difficult to replicate elsewhere. But these local organizations conciliated working-class opinion by providing supporters with clearly defined but safely subordinate roles which reinforced their identification with the party and encouraged the building of bridges across class boundaries. And in 1877 the National Liberal Federation formed an umbrella organization for them. These processes were beginning before 1867, but the Second Reform Act made their cumulative acceleration inescapable, especially in the larger boroughs. Working-class activists were firmly harnessed to the major parties by these means, leaving less room than ever for the development of popular political alternatives.

The main parties' concern to attach the new voters to the existing system was pursued more through organization and assimilation than through policies. Contrary to Bagehot's expectations, the parties did not compete ruinously for the favour of the working-class electorate. They did not need to do so. In the fragmentary and undeveloped state of working-class political organizations and ideology, the orthodox views on how economy and society ought to work went effectively unchallenged from below. None of the governments between 1868 and 1885 were demonstrably deflected in their aims by any perceived need to conciliate working-class opinion or fend off socialism. Even Disraeli's famous reforming ministry of 1874–80 turns out to have had no overall strategy or philosophy, and to have followed a path dictated by administrative inertia and expediency, even in the field of public health. The trade union legislation of 1875 is perhaps the only case of a government yielding to pressure from organized labour on a class-based issue. Changes in the presentation of policy were more important. Party leaders began to display themselves to provincial electors in great set-piece speeches before massed audiences, as in Disraeli's triumphant visit to Manchester

46

in 1872 and Gladstone's famous Midlothian campaign of 1879–80 against Turkish atrocities in Bulgaria. These events invited celebratory audience participation and invoked a sense of popular theatre and ritual, which helps to explain the tolerance of working-class crowds for seemingly endless speeches. The burgeoning popular press advertised and reinforced these occasions, and spread their messages to a wider public. Here again, these trends were emerging before 1867, but the new electoral system encouraged their full flowering.

Older kinds of popular political ritual were a long time dying in the new climate, however. The importance of the drink interest was if anything reinforced by the further spread of the vote among the 'drinking classes', and the politicization of the publican was accentuated by Gladstone's restrictive licensing legislation of 1869 and 1872, which reinforced and extended the widespread alliance between brewers, publicans and Tories. Closely related to this was the persistence of bribery and 'treating', which were still notoriously frequent at the 1880 election and were only reduced to tolerable proportions by the Corrupt Practices Act of 1883. In this respect, as in others, the Ballot Act alone did not have the expected results. Nor did the tradition of election riots, often involving serious threats to life, property and dignity, subside: they remained lively and endemic in 1885, and the police were often quite unable to control them. But the rioters divided along established party lines, with strong overtones of simple letting-off of steam during an accepted period of license. As Richter remarks, 'The prevailing Victorian attitude toward electoral rambunctiousness [sic] was singularly cavalier.' This was itself significant, as *The Times* commented in 1885,

> The country was able without danger to act as if it were momentarily insane because it felt itself essentially sane at bottom. A nation without settled political instincts and habits could not have let itself run wild, as has been the recent pleasure of Englishmen. . . . A good fight at intervals of four or five or six years is all very well.

No better indication could be found of the success with which the established political parties managed the new electorate of 1867 and assimilated it to the existing political system, adapting judiciously to new needs while perpetuating traditional patterns of behaviour.

All this tends to confirm Frederic Harrison's scepticism about the real impact of the Second Reform Act, in the short and medium term, on those whom it enfranchised. As he said,

> What is wanted is, not to give men votes, but to give them power. The grand object of the 'constitutional' and 'culture' factions is to create a Bill which shall appear to create a great many new votes, but really create no new influence.
>
> (1975, 161)

And indeed, Bagehot's manual for keeping dangerous items off the political agenda and minimizing change was faithfully expressed in the course of events, while Arnold, too, can have found little to worry him. What changes there were involved the strengthening of the Conservative and Liberal hold upon parliamentary politics, the firming-up of party lines and the squeezing-out of independents, and the alternation of strong party governments with professed programmes rather than the centrist square-dance of overlapping coalitions which marked the mid-Victorian years. Governments became stronger, and the House of Commons acquired enhanced legitimacy, without the social structure of parliament or Cabinets changing in any significant way, and without the new voters being able to translate their votes into real influence on the legislative process. The Second Reform Act helped to remake the Conservative Party as a credible party of government, and enabled Disraeli to conjure up his reputation as the founder of the modern Conservative Party, but it did little or nothing for the new voters whose expectations, pretensions and qualities were so much discussed in the debates of 1866–7. It neither prevented revolution, nor did it bring about startling changes in the British political system. In the light of contemporary forebodings, what seems remarkable is how little difference it actually made.

In the long run, however, the significance of the Second Reform Act was arguably much greater. It may not actually have prevented revolution, but it defused the emergent grievances of an organized working class with articulate leaders and spokesmen from the industrial and professional middle class, and it assimiliated them into the existing two-party system before they had fully developed separate political institutions of their own. The stability with which the transition to the new system was accomplished no doubt helped to make the introduction of the secret ballot more acceptable, and certainly paved the way for the extension of household suffrage into the counties in the Third Reform Act of 1884. Significantly, perhaps, matters went no further until after the First World War. The 1867 Act enfranchised householders: stable residents, usually of mature years, with some stake, however limited, in their communities. The 'residuum' – the disreputable working class – who inspired so much fear and loathing in the reform debates, were in practice most unlikely to qualify for the vote, or to use it. There was no subsequent move to extend voting rights beyond the principles of 1867, and the eventual rise of unskilled unions, socialist organizations and the Labour Party can have done little to encourage politicans to move in this direction. So British 'democracy' remained very limited in practice: certainly a long way short of manhood suffrage in parliamentary elections. Herein, perhaps, lies the most important consequence of the Second Reform Act. It provided the basis for an enduring and relatively uncontroversial settlement of the franchise question, removing a contentious issue from the political arena before it became dangerous to the existing structure of power and property, and enabling the politically articulate working class to become (often enthusiastic) accomplices and participants in the party political game. The rise of the Labour Party, after all, was seriously impeded by the difficulty of detaching supporters from one or other of the major parties. A disappointed Engels had commented in 1868 that 'Everywhere the proletariat is the rag, tag and bobtail of the official parties, and if any party has gained strength from the new voters, it is the Tories.' This double outcome proved largely true in the long run as well as in the short; and while we cannot assume that Disraeli planned for or predicted this doubly gratifying result, we can be sure that he would have been delighted by the stability and durability of his opportunistic legislation, and by the many years of Conservative government that followed in its wake, especially in the late nineteenth and early twentieth centuries.

Bibliography

Place of publication is London unless otherwise stated.

H. Ausubel, *John Bright, Victorian Reformer* (1966).

Walter Bagehot, *The English Constitution* (1872 edn).

R. Blake, *Disraeli* (paperback edn, 1969).

C. Brent, 'The immediate impact of the Second Reform Act on a southern county town: voting patterns at Lewes Borough in 1865 and 1868', *Southern History* 2 (1980), 129–77.

M. Cowling, *1867: Disraeli, Gladstone and Revolution* (Cambridge, 1967).

R. W. Davis, *Political Change and Continuity, 1760–1885: A Buckinghamshire Study* (Newton Abbot, 1972).

H. I. Dutton and J. E. King, 'The Limits of Paternalism the Cotton Tyrants of North Lancashire, 1836–54', *Social History* 7 (1982), 59–74.

E. J. Evans, *The Forging of the Modern State, 1783–1870* (1983).

E. J. Feuchtwanger, *Democracy and Empire* (1985).

E. J. Feuchtwanger, *Disraeli, Democracy and the Tory Party* (1968).

E. J. Feuchtwanger, *Gladstone* (1975).

D. Fraser, *Urban Politics in Victorian England* (Leicester, 1976).

J. Garrard, 'Parties, members and voters after 1867: a local study', *Historical Journal* 20 (1977), 145–63.

H. J. Hanham, *Elections and Party Management* (1959).

Frederic Harrison, *Order and Progress* (1875, reprinted Hassocks, 1975).

Royden Harrison, *Before the Socialists* (1965).

G. Himmelfarb, 'The politics of democracy: the English Reform Act of 1867', *Journal of British Studies* 6 (1966), 97–138.

K. T. Hoppen, 'The franchise and electoral politics in England and Ireland 1832–85', *History* 70 (1985), 202–17.

P. Joyce, *Work, Society and Politics* (Hassocks, 1980).

C. Kent, *Brains and Numbers: Elitism, Comtism and Democracy in Mid-Victorian England* (1978).

N. Kirk, *The Growth of Working-Class Reformism in Mid-Victorian England* (1985).

J. C. Lowe, 'The Tory triumph of 1868 in Blackburn and in Lancashire', *Historical Journal* 16 (1973), 733–48.

K. Marx and F. Engels, *Articles on Britain* (Moscow, 1971).

K. Marx and F. Engels, *Correspondence 1846–95* (1934).

D. C. Moore, *The Politics of Deference* (Hassocks, 1976).

R. S. Neale, *Class and Ideology in the Nineteenth Century* (1973).

T. Nossiter, *Influence, Opinion and Political Idioms in Reformed England* (Hassocks, 1975).

C. O'Leary, *The Elimination of Corrupt Practices in British Elections, 1868–1911* (Oxford, 1962).

J. Prest, *Lord John Russell* (1972).

D. Richter, *Riotous Victorians* (Athens, Ohio, 1981).

J. Ruskin, *Unto This Last, and Other Essays on Art and Political Economy* (Everyman edn, 1907).

N. St John-Stevas, *Walter Bagehot* (1959).

C. Seymour, *Electoral Reform in England and Wales* (1915, reprinted Newton Abbot, 1970).

F. B. Smith, 'The "dependence of license upon faith": Miss Gertrude Himmelfarb on the Second Reform Act', *Journal of British Studies* 7 (1967), 96–9; and Himmelfarb's reply, 100–4.

F. B. Smith, *The Making of the Second Reform Bill* (Cambridge, 1966).

P. Smith, *Disraelian Conservatism and Social Reform* (1967).

T. R. Tholfsen, *Working-class Radicalism in Mid-Victorian England* (1976).

J. R. Vincent, 'The effect of the Second Reform Act in Lancashire', *Historical Journal* 11 (1968), 84–94.

J. R. Vincent, *The Formation of the Liberal Party, 1857–68* (1966).

J. R. Vincent, *Poll-books: How Victorians Voted* (Cambridge, 1967).

J. R. Vincent (ed.), *Disraeli, Derby and the Conservative Party* (Hassocks, 1978).

D. G. Wright, *Democracy and Reform, 1815–85* (1970).